HOW TO TALK TO A TIGER...
AND OTHER ANIMALS

HOW CRITTERS COMMUNICATE IN THE WILD

written by
JASON BITTEL

illustrated by
KELSEY BUZZELL

MAGIC CAT PUBLISHING

NEW YORK

If you are anything like the average person, by the end of today you will have said around 7,000 words. I'll bet there were lots of reasons for saying those words. Perhaps you asked someone to pass the milk at breakfast. Maybe you shouted at a cyclist who sped past you in the crosswalk on your way into school. Perhaps you told your mom you loved her when you headed through the door, and maybe you even shared your homework with a friend.

While animals haven't developed all the words that humans have, they still have many of the same reasons for communicating as you do—to get food, to protect themselves from dangerous situations, to show affection, or to help one another out. But animals—and the habitats they live in—vary enormously, and so do the means by which they have learned to communicate. Some are strange, some even verge on silly . . . but all of them serve a vital purpose: to ensure the creature's own survival and, ultimately, the survival of its species. Fish, quite literally, fart for their lives. And that's a fact.

CONTENTS

SIGHTS

SO, YOU WANT TO TALK TO A TIGER?

Tigers communicate with each other in a variety of ways, including with sounds, scents, and touches. But you can learn most of what you need to know by watching a tiger's tail.

Tigers are the largest cats on Earth, and as such, their tails can stretch out 3 feet in length. If a tiger's tail is held high and softly swishing, the animal is interested in being social. Perhaps it's exploring a new area or making contact with another tiger for mating purposes. If the tail is held low and loose, then the tiger is relaxed and calm. But if that tail starts to THRASH or TWITCH from left to right—then watch out! This means the tiger is scared, nervous, or displaying aggression.

AN OPEN MOUTH, A CHEST BEAT, A PUFFED-UP STANCE: ASSERTING YOURSELF THROUGH BODY LANGUAGE

→ Great white sharks tell each other to back off by opening their mouths at one another, which scientists call **GAPING**. They often gape at the time of feeding, driven by frenzy, and are more likely to physically attack then than when defending their territory.

→ The silverback gorilla's most famous gesture is the **CHEST BEAT**—it stands on two legs and hits its chest alternately with open hands. The gorilla starts off hooting, sometimes biting off a leaf, then the hoots speed up until they slur together. Then, it stands up and does a quick chest beat, finishing off the display by hitting the ground.

→ Male giraffes make their dominance known by **STANDING AS TALL AS POSSIBLE**, with stiff, straight necks and locked legs. When the giraffes show submissive behavior, the head and ears are held down.

A TORTOISE STAND-OFF

Galápagos tortoises are huge, hulking reptiles with a slow, plodding way of life, but they will engage in dominance poses when it's time to mate or even to decide who gets the right-of-way on a narrow path. When two males go up against one another, each will try to stick its neck and head way up into the air. Then, they both slowly let their heads lower, before going back up again and again. And it can go on like this—two tortoises in the middle of the road, stuck in a slow-motion staring contest—until one tortoise is able to crane its neck higher than the other. **SLOW AND STEADY MAY WIN THE RACE, BUT THE HEAD HELD HIGHER WINS THE ROAD.**

THE TICKLE-ME-LORIS IS ADORABLE AND DEADLY

Lorises are one of the cutest animals on Earth. These forest primates are small enough to fit in your pocket and have large puppy dog eyes. In recent years, lorises have been taken out of the wild and sold as pets. Some have even found their way onto the internet. Videos show the animal lifting its arms above its head and leaning backwards as its owner rubs and scratches its belly. **IT LOOKS LIKE THE LORIS IS ENJOYING ITSELF, BUT LOOKS CAN BE DECEIVING** . . . especially if you don't speak loris. Scientists say that a loris with its arms held over its head is showing that it feels threatened and will defend itself if necessary.

Each loris has a pair of secret weapons: **SPECIALIZED GLANDS**. These glands are on their inner elbows and produce a clear, smelly liquid that can cause an allergic reaction in humans. Interestingly, because the oil is on the loris's elbows, it has to first lick it to mix it with saliva, then bite its victim for the toxins to release. This explains why a scared loris would put its arms up—**IT'S GETTING ITS VENOM GLANDS CLOSE TO ITS MOUTH IN CASE IT NEEDS TO FIGHT.**

 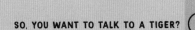

IT'S GOOD TO BE TOP DOG →

Most people don't spend enough time in the ocean to learn about stingray behavior. And not everyone can afford to go on a wildlife safari to watch a lion's daily routine. But there are animals living inside many of our homes that we get to see every day: our pets. And even with names like Fido, Fifi, and Mr. Snicklefritz, their behaviors still reflect the wild animals that lurk within. The saying "It's not the size of the dog in the fight, it's the size of the fight in the dog" is true to some extent. Size is important in battles between dogs that want to be in charge, but it's not the only factor—which won't be surprising to anyone who has a yappy little dog at home.

→ Have you ever been around two dogs that seem to be running around and playing just fine until one of them decides it's had enough and starts to snarl? It can happen so fast, even the other dog seems surprised. This is how dogs communicate. Some of it is straightforward: The dog that's baring its teeth and growling is annoyed, tired, or perhaps it wants to be left alone. BUT IT'S EASY TO MISS WHAT IT MIGHT BE SAYING BECAUSE A LOT OF WHAT'S BEING COMMUNICATED HAPPENS THROUGH BODY LANGUAGE.

→ Look at a dog's **TAIL**. Is it stiff and raised? That signals aggression. Or is it limp and tucked between the legs? This is a sign that the dog wants to submit.

→ The **EARS** of a dog are important. If their ears are erect, it can mean that it's alert, but it can also hint at aggression. And if the ears are laid back against the head, it means that the dog is afraid.

→ **A DOG'S SIGNALS CAN ALL MIX TOGETHER TO MEAN DIFFERENT THINGS.** For example, a dog with its ears and tail straight up might be showing how tough it is to another dog. But a dog with its ears flat against its head and its tail between its legs can also be dangerous. This signals that the animal feels threatened, and while it might be trying to avoid trouble by backing away, it is also saying that it can attack if necessary.

THE FOUR-YEAR CHIMP WAR

When scientist Jane Goodall first started studying the chimpanzees of Tanzania, she believed that the animals were kinder than humans. But in 1974, Goodall saw something to challenge her belief . . .

Chimpanzees are smart animals, and they live in troops that can include up to 150 individuals, led by a single male known as the alpha. Alpha males have better access to food, grooming, and mates, but the position also comes with risks, as other males try to overthrow the alpha. Chimpanzees can invade another group's territory and target its leading males. If the conquerors succeed in driving off or dispatching the other males, then they can take that forest for their own, which is what Jane witnessed.

Over the course of four years, Jane watched as chimpanzees from a group known as the Kasakela came out of the southern part of the forest and launched attacks on a group called the Kahama in the north. Eventually, the Kasakela won the war, but were then forced to retreat back to their original position when an even larger group known as the Kalande took over the land they'd just won! Goodall called it the Gombe Chimpanzee War and learned that **EVEN THE SMARTEST WILD ANIMALS CAN'T ALWAYS USE COMMUNICATION TO AVOID CONFLICT.**

DO THE WAGGLE! ↓

If a honeybee is buzzing around out in the world and it discovers a really tasty patch of flowers or a nice place for a new nest, it might fly back to its hive to convince other bees to follow it. But there's just one problem—how does a bee tell another bee where to go? This question stumped researchers for a long time. After all, bees are small, and the world is so big. And even though the insects live together, nobody could explain how an insect could pass along complicated information.

But in the 1920s, an Austrian scientist named Karl von Frisch made a discovery. HONEYBEES TELL EACH OTHER WHERE TO GO BY DANCING IN HIGHLY COMPLEX FIGURE-EIGHT PATTERNS, LIKE TINY, FURRY ICE SKATERS.

→ The harder and longer a bee dances, the more confident it is about the message it's trying to send. So, when other bees notice that a bee is waggling, they tend to join up with it and start waggling nearby. SLOWLY BUT SURELY, THIS MESSAGE SPREADS THROUGHOUT THE COLONY, and the momentum causes other bees that might also be waggling to give up on their waggles. Eventually, enough bees will be moving in figure-eight patterns that a decision can be reached, and the bees will set out to find what got the first bee so excited.

→ According to Karl von Frisch and many scientists who have come after him, THE WAGGLE DANCE ISN'T JUST ABOUT CONVINCING OTHER BEES—IT ALSO CONTAINS DIRECTIONS. Using a system of angles and relation to where the sun is in the sky, that first pathfinder honeybee can guide her sisters in the general direction of the flowers or new nest. They will even change the direction of their dance as the day goes on, to account for the movement of the sun!

→ Honeybees sometimes lace flowers with **CHEMICALS KNOWN AS PHEROMONES**. This allows other bees who are farther away to sniff them out. They use the smell like street signs that tell them where to go.

→ Scientists have been studying honeybee signals for hundreds of years and are still not exactly sure how it all works. All they know is that an insect the size of a pencil eraser is able give and follow directions on a regular basis, **ALL THROUGH SHAKING ITS LITTLE BEE BUTT.**

30°

DIRECTION TO FLOWERS

PEACOCK SPIDERS DANCE FOR THEIR LIVES

A male peacock spider no bigger than a grain of rice launches himself into the air and lands beside a female on a nearby leaf. She turns and looks at him with all eight of her eyes. If he doesn't do something quickly, the female will strike and gobble him up. So, what is a male peacock spider to do? Fight? Run? Hide?

DANCE! The male spider lifts one of his front legs into the air and starts to wiggle it. Then, he adds another leg from the other side of his body and begins to move the two limbs in a rhythm. Like a conductor leading an orchestra, the spider waves his arms back and forth, up and down, in a pattern only he and she recognize.

As the male continues to whip and twitch his legs back and forth, he raises up his neon abdomen and starts to shake it to the beat. With its reds, oranges, purples and greens, the spider's backside is **MESMERIZING**. Slowly, the male gets closer to the female . . . And closer . . . Then, he grabs onto her with his dancing legs and wraps her up in an embrace. The female has accepted him as a mate. Phew!

DANCING IS FOR THE BIRDS ↓

Every year, Andean flamingos fly hundreds of miles to salt lakes in the mountains of South America, where they dip their beaks into the water to find plantlike creatures called diatoms. But the local cuisine isn't why the flamingos have flocked . . . They're ready to dance!

Flamingo courtship is a group activity where around fifty birds come together in a tightly packed group and begin walking through the water. Then, all at the same time, some of the birds turn their large, black bills to the left, while others turn theirs to the right. Then, they switch. While their legs are obviously moving to carry them across the water, the birds keep their bodies perfectly still. **THE WHOLE FLOCK LOOKS LIKE THEY ARE FLOATING,** with their heads jerking back and forth like serious tango dancers.

THE RISING SUN: A SAGE GROUSE

A sage grouse is a little bird that lives in the United States and Canada. The male of this species has long, spikelike feathers on its tail that it spreads out to create what **LOOKS LIKE A RISING SUN**. It also has two sacs of bare, featherless skin on either side of its throat, and when it wants to try to impress a female, it will rapidly inflate and deflate those sacs with air, creating a distinct *BOOM* sound.

LOVE IS IN THE WATER: THE CLARK'S GREBE

Clark's grebes dance to determine who they mate with for life or to re-establish the bond for birds who have already paired up. The dance includes swimming side by side while flicking water in each other's faces, taking turns preening the feathers on their backs, and even offering each other a gift of fish. But the best part comes at the end, when each grebe raises its head into the air, puts its wings behind its back, and starts **RUNNING ACROSS THE SURFACE OF THE WATER IN PERFECT UNISON.**

FLAMBOYANT FEATHERS: THE GREATER BIRD-OF-PARADISE

→ Some people make a statement with the clothes they wear . . . and a family of birds native to New Guinea and northeastern Australia do the same with their **FEATHERS**: the birds-of-paradise.

→ The feathers on the head of the male greater bird-of-paradise are very unique. They have almost no barbs, which help birds to fly. Instead, these feathers look more like wires with small tufts at the ends. These changes serve to **IMPROVE THE MALE'S CHANCES** during courtship.

→ The male greater bird-of-paradise has reddish feathers covering most of its body and a **LONG TUFT** of lighter, yellow feathers in the middle of its back.

→ When a female comes into view, **MALES COMPETE** with each other by stretching their wings out wide, fluffing up their tuft, and hopping along a branch while squawking.

→ The tufts are so big that the bird looks like a bunch of **FEATHER DUSTERS** dancing around in the forest canopy.

IF LOOKS COULD KILL →

When a jackdaw looks your way, it's impossible not to take notice. This is because, unlike the other birds in its family, like the dark-eyed crows and rooks, jackdaws sport a pair of brilliant WHITE PEEPERS WITH SMALL BLACK PUPILS. And this has made scientists wonder if these big eyeballs serve a purpose.

So, in 2014, researchers placed pictures of four different kinds of eyeballs at the back of 100 nest boxes outside of Cambridge, England. Importantly, the scientists also put cameras inside the nest boxes, so they could see how the jackdaws reacted to seeing the eyes, some of which were big and white like their own, while others were small and black like their cousins'.

→ When the birds landed and peeked inside a nest box with black eyes unlike their own, they had no problem hanging around and even building a nest inside. But if the birds looked inside and saw a pair of white, jackdaw-like eyes staring back at them, **THEY WERE MORE LIKELY TO FLY AWAY.**

→ According to the scientists, this may mean that jackdaws engage in **STARING CONTESTS** to decide who gets to keep a nest. This makes logical sense, too, since it's better for the birds to settle things with a flash of an eyeball than with a peck of a beak, which could lead to serious injuries.

→ Jackdaws are special among the crow family in that they nest in natural hollows in trees, as well as cavities in walls and chimneys. Jackdaws cannot create their own nest areas, as some woodpeckers do, so they have to **COMPETE WITH OTHERS** for a limited resource. And, because jackdaws nest close to one another, there is a fight to gain the best spot.

→ If this is true, the study would mean **JACKDAWS ARE THE FIRST NON-PRIMATES KNOWN TO COMMUNICATE USING THEIR EYES.** And who knows what else they might be capable of saying? We humans say plenty with our eyes, of course. Just think of how much one stern stare from your parent means, without them having to say anything at all!

EYES ARE THE GATEWAY TO THE PRIMATE SOUL

When a younger chimpanzee wants to eat something a more dominant chimp is chowing down upon, the pipsqueak will stare at the food intently. And when a macaque wants to tell another monkey that it means no harm, it will stare off into the distance. These are just some of the many ways primates have evolved to **USE THEIR EYES TO TALK TO ONE ANOTHER**.

Look at your own eyes in the mirror and you'll notice a large, white part of your eyeball. This is called the sclera. Most animals do not have the same kind of scleras as we do—check out the eyes of your pet dog, cat, hamster, lorikeet, or goldfish. See the difference? While it used to be thought that humans were the only primates that developed white scleras, more recent studies have found that most gorillas also have whites in their eyes. Scientists also found that chimps, bonobos, and orangutans all had whiter eyes than we originally thought. **WHO KNOWS WHAT ELSE WE'LL FIND NOW THAT WE KNOW WHERE TO LOOK?**

PLAYING POSSUM ↓

A hungry coyote scampers through the forests in search of a meal. It's been days since the animal last ate, and finally, its patience is rewarded as it spots a medium-size mammal waddling on the path ahead. It's an opossum, the coyote realizes . . . Yum! Opossums are no match for a coyote—they don't have big teeth, nor claws, nor venom, nor spines—and so the coyote attacks.

But as soon as the coyote's teeth sink into North America's only marsupial, the opossum goes limp. Not only that, but the opossum's eyes roll back into its head, drool pours out of its mouth, its ears start twitching, and it poops everywhere. The coyote persists, and that's when a nasty, foul-smelling, green goo squirts out of a pair of glands on the opossum's bottom. The coyote takes a whiff. And gags. And runs away. After a while, the opossum rolls back onto its feet and goes about its day. This is known as death-feigning. Playing dead. And it's all an act. A clever ruse that allows the lowly opossum to beat a predator many times its size.

STAR TURN

When hognose snakes are threatened by a predator, these small, squat snakes first puff up and try to make themselves appear larger. They also hiss loudly and bite the air. But if that doesn't scare off whatever's bothering them, hognose snakes have another trick. All at once, the serpents flip onto their backs, exposing their creamy white bellies, and **BEGIN TO WRITHE** like they've just been tossed into a frying pan. Their **MOUTHS GAPE WIDE,** and their **TONGUES WRIGGLE AND THRASH,** and then, they coil up into a ball and become still. This death-feigning is an Oscar-worthy performance.

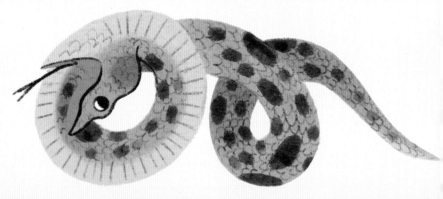

LADYBUGS
are capable fliers, for instance, but they'd rather tuck their legs in and play dead when you try to catch them. They also sometimes push out a smelly, yellow liquid that works just like the opossum's green one.

→ While it's not a classic form of communication, feigning death does send information from one animal to another. It's the opossum's way of telling the coyote that it will not like how it tastes. You can watch this same scenario play out with animals in your garden . . .

When playing dead, **FIRE-BELLIED TOADS** arch their backs and twist their limbs to display yellow or orange warning markings on the undersides of their feet. They sometimes flip onto their backs to show similar markings on their underside—which explains the name "fire-bellied."

When a male **NURSERY WEB SPIDER** brings his date a juicy insect as a present, sometimes the female will try to eat him instead! To avoid this, the male pretends he's dead while clutching onto the insect, so that when the female drags the bug away, he tags along for the ride. Perhaps once she has a full belly, the female will be more likely to mate with him than kill him.

FAKE DEATH = FLAVORSOME DINNER

Cichlids, an African fish, use death-feigning to their advantage. These critters can be found **LYING MOTIONLESS** on the bottom of a lake, their skin splotchy and looking slightly rotten. When another fish comes by hoping to take a bite of what it thinks is a free meal, the cichlid "comes back to life" and gulps the minnow down.

WHERE THE SUN DOESN'T SHINE →

The ocean is a deep, murky place. And it gets dark a lot faster than you think. If you turn the Eiffel Tower upside down and dip it in the sea, nearly all of the sun's rays would be gone before you sunk past the structure's tip.

It's a black, cold, dangerous world down there in what scientists call the midnight zone, where light never reaches. But surprisingly, this world is humming with life. And even here, animals have found ways to communicate with each other.

One deep sea method of communication is bioluminescence. Yes, just like the chemical reaction that lights up a glowworm's rear end, fish, squid, and tons of other critters have evolved the ability to create their own light. In fact, scientists believe 76 percent of all ocean animals can produce light in one way or another—that's three out of every four ocean creatures!

→ **OSTRACODS**, or **FIREFLEAS**, are like the lightning bugs of the deep. These tiny crustaceans flit around as they light up, sometimes flashing in a sequence designed to impress the female firefleas.

→ **ANGLERFISH**, flashlight fish, and ponyfish all use light when it comes to mating, but their displays are simpler than firefleas'. As in, these fish use light simply as a way to find members of their own species in the dark, which is no easy task. The lights are also thought to help the fish tell the difference between males and females.

→ Most light down below is of the blue variety, but a few fish have figured out how to glow red. The deep-sea **DRAGONFISH** is one of these, and it's not a fish you'd want to run into in the dark! They have teeth so big and sharp they don't even fit inside their mouths. The good news is they're only 6 inches long. Dragonfish create red light using a special organ known as a photophore. Scientists believe the animals use this blinker not only to lure in prey, but also as a way to show other dragonfish prey that might be nearby, which is actually quite neighborly.

FIRE IN THE WAVES

A few days after the full moon, and an hour after sunset, if you take a boat out into the waters surrounding the islands of Bermuda, you just might catch a flicker of fire below the waves. Christopher Columbus was lucky enough to see the lights in 1492. He compared them to "the flame of a small candle alternately raised and lowered." **BUT THESE ELECTRIC BLUE FLAMES ARE ACTUALLY BERMUDA FIREWORMS.**

Fireworms spend most of their lives living on the seabed, hidden away inside tubes made of their own spit, called mucus. But about once a month, they leave their hideaways in order to breed. After the sun goes down, the females wriggle their way up to the water's surface where they dance about and leak a glowing, green-blue chemical. Once the males see it, they come shooting up from the depths. As they reach the females, the males start doing their own underwater dance, emitting neon teal flashes. And when enough fireworms get together, every fireworm begins releasing its reproductive cells to create new fireworms. After that, each one sinks down to the ocean floor where it will eat and hide for another lunar cycle, at which point the festivities will begin again.

SPEAKING IN HUES →

In nature, colors are essential for communication between animal species. A little flash of a feather here or a tinted tuft of fur there can mean the difference between life and death.

Gelada baboons live in family groups that can include up to 350 baboons. And with so many monkeys running around, it's important to avoid deadly fights. One way gelada baboons do this is by advertising strength through color.

→ Like most primates, geladas are covered in fur. But there's a curious exception on their chests, where **ONE PATCH IS LEFT HAIRLESS** in the shape of an hourglass. In males, this spot can range from pink to ruby red.

→ A fiery red patch on a female shows a male that she is ready to mate. A male gelada displays a red heart-shaped patch that is more brightly colored when they have access to reproductive females. This has earned them the nickname, **BLEEDING-HEART BABOONS**.

→ Scientists have found that there's a link between a male gelada's status in the group and the hue it sports on its chest. Bigger, more successful males tend to have brighter chest patches. It's almost as if these monkeys are wearing a red sign that says to the kingdom, **"YOU BETTER NOT MESS WITH ME!"**

SHAKE YOUR TAIL FEATHERS

Some colors are meant to impress rather than intimidate. The peacock has evolved gigantic, gorgeous plumes of tail feathers that shimmer when they give them a shake. Scientists still aren't completely sure why peacocks have such huge tail feathers. Most people, including Charles Darwin, believe that the feathers are a way for the males to outcompete each other in an attempt to woo a female. But another theory says the tails are a badge of survival.

A peacock's tail can be more than 5 feet long. And all that extra baggage has to make it harder for the males to find food, avoid predators, and generally just live their lives. So, some scientists believe that a big, beautiful tail display is the peacock's way of showing peahens that he has really good genes, simply because he's been able to survive while sporting a handicap on his backside.

It's clear that the peacock is saying something with his tail, but **SCIENTISTS ARE STILL TRYING TO FIGURE OUT EXACTLY WHAT THAT MESSAGE IS**. The uncertainty is almost inspiring in a way . . .

Even when it seems like everything has been discovered about the animal kingdom, plenty of mystery remains.

FLASHING MESSAGES

Wave to the left. Now, using your other hand, wave to the right. Now imagine that you could do both of these things at the same time, using only your skin. This is what it's like to be a Caribbean reef squid.

These marvelous little squids have plenty of arms and tentacles, and yet, they communicate with each other by **FLASHING MESSAGES ACROSS THE SURFACE OF THEIR SLIPPERY SKIN**. Squid are able to perform these interesting displays thanks to special organs called chromatophores, which are controlled by tiny muscles. When the muscles flex, the chromatophores are cinched down into tiny dots, but when they release, the spots open wide into splotches of color. And when hundreds or even thousands of these organs start firing at once, the effect can be dazzling.

Squid can produce all kinds of patterns on their skin. One well-known example looks like zebra stripes, which are used to compete with other squid during mating. When the squid are in danger, their eyebrows turn golden and their arms turn white. They may also use their chromatophores to create a series of large eyespots on their body that can scare a predator away.

LOOK, BUT DON'T TOUCH! ↓

Is there a more recognizable animal than a skunk? Black body. White stripes. Stinky odor. But did you know that the white stripes are linked to the stinky odor? It's called aposematic coloration, which means WARNING COLORS.

From the neon blue circles on a highly venomous blue-ringed octopus to the bright orange markings of a monarch butterfly, examples of aposematic coloration flourish across the animal kingdom. The ladybug's and glowworm's spots are aposematic, as are the stripes on a lionfish and on many different kinds of wasps and bees.

Warning signals are handy quirks of evolution; THEY HELP PREY ANIMALS TO AVOID BEING EATEN, AND THEY HELP PREDATORS TO AVOID HAVING THEIR DAY RUINED.

The bright red fuzz on a velvet ant's back warns of its powerful sting, while poison dart frogs come in an array of brilliant blues, yellows, greens, and oranges as a way to notify predators that eating one could result in their last meal on Earth!

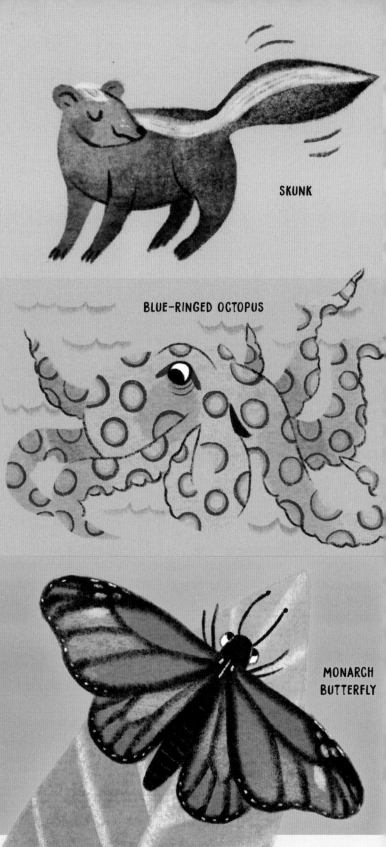

SKUNK

BLUE-RINGED OCTOPUS

MONARCH BUTTERFLY

COPYCATS, MIMICS, AND IMPOSTERS

There's a whole host of edible animals that are protected by their resemblance to one avoided by predators. This is called Batesian mimicry, after a scientist named Henry Walter Bates who discovered the first known case of such mimicry while studying butterflies in the rainforests of Brazil.

Masters of Batesian mimicry include the HOVERFLIES. There are around 6,000 species of hoverfly, cousins to the houseflies that buzz around your kitchen. But many species of hoverfly don't look like a fly at all. They look like bees. In fact, it is so convincing that there's a good chance that you've run away from a hoverfly before because you were worried that you were about to get stung. Of course, hoverflies can't sting at all.

MIMICRY allows these species to benefit from the advantages of poisonous glands and venomous stingers without actually having to invest nutrients toward making such defensive weapons. It's another awe-inspiring way animals have evolved to avoid turning into someone else's meal.

LADYBUG

VELVET ANT

LIONFISH

POISON DART FROG

WASP

→ **YOU MAY BE WONDERING WHY SOME APOSEMATIC ANIMALS ARE BLACK AND WHITE WHILE OTHERS ARE VIBRANTLY COLORED.** Well, the coloration varies on the animal's lifestyle. Colorful animals like the bumblebee and the coral snake tend to be active during the day, when predators with eyes best suited to daylight might be able to notice their colorations and choose to stay away. But animals like the skunk, porcupine, and honey badger do most of their foraging at night, when black and white patterns are most easily seen by predators that make use of night vision.

The **CLEARWING SPHINX MOTH** is a large, buzzing species commonly mistaken for a bee, even though it acts more like a hummingbird. Some mantidflies also sport the yellow and black getup of wasps, though they, too, lack the ability to sting. There's even a bee beetle which hails from the scarab family but has markings that make it look like something far more dangerous.

Venomous coral snakes are mimicked by harmless ground snakes and scarlet kingsnakes. Usually meek katydids have been found mimicking formidable tiger beetles. And there are even insects from the genus *Prosoplecta* that have shiny red shells and black spots that make them look like adorable ladybugs. But they're not ladybugs. They're **COCKROACHES**. Eek!

TEAMWORK MAKES THE DREAM WORK→

At 3 feet long, the roving coral grouper is a large, fast fish with a mouth like a vacuum. And when it's hungry, it chases smaller fish out into the open water and gulps them down whole. But sometimes, small fish can elude their vacuum jaws by diving down into one of the many cracks found in the coral reef below. So, rather than give up on a fish out of reach, the grouper calls for backup.

First, the grouper positions its body vertically, with its snout pointing at the hidden fish's location like the tip of an arrow. Then, it starts to shake its head vigorously. A pause . . . then a shake. Another pause . . . another shake.

→ GROUPERS HAVE BEEN KNOWN TO HUNT COOPERATIVELY with other species of fish, each with unique skill sets that, when used in combination, allow the hunters to extract their prize.

→ The HUMPHEAD WRASSE has a powerful beak that it uses to chomp through coral. Together with the grouper and giant moray eel it forms a team, each able to offer something that the others cannot, and they catch more food together than they could alone.

A LITTLE DROP OF HONEY

Planthopper insects spend their days in the trees, with their mouthparts plunged in the bark, slurping out juice. To these tiny sapsuckers, pretty much everything in the forests of Madagascar wants to eat you. So, when a hungry day gecko, with its powerful, projectile tongue, discovers a planthopper, you might expect it to be "game over." In fact, the game is just beginning.

The day gecko starts to bob its head. In turn, the planthopper begins to vibrate its backside. After a while, the bug SQUIRTS A TINY DROP OF HONEYDEW into the day gecko's mouth, which the lizard happily licks up.

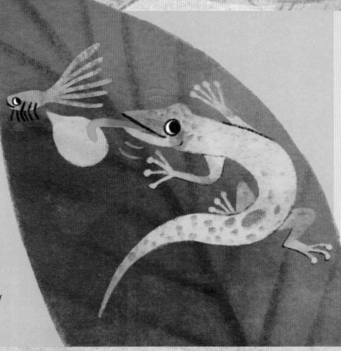

COME AND GET IT!

Fish on a coral reef have to constantly fend off tiny, bloodsucking parasites called isopods. Lucky for them, there are other fish who are willing to help out.

A bigger fish, like a shark or ray, will spread out its fins, open its mouth, flare its gills, and then remain perfectly still. This is the bigger fish's way of saying, "I'M LOOKING TO BE CLEANED." In response, a bunch of smaller creatures, like wrasses and shrimp, will begin to pick at its little bits of dead skin and parasites. The bigger fish gets rid of all its parasites and the smaller fish and shrimp get an easy meal— everybody wins!

→ The **GIANT MORAY EEL** is a long, lithe acrobat that can poke around in cracks much too small for the grouper to access.

→ A grouper will also recruit the help of a giant moray eel before it has found something it wants to eat. Scientists have observed the grouper hanging outside the entrance of a giant moray eel's den and **PERFORMING REPEATED SHIMMIES.** Sometimes the eel just stays put. But other times, it comes out to play and the two animals can be seen swimming off together, looking for trouble.

KOKO THE GORILLA LEARNS TO SIGN

In 1971, Koko, a western lowland gorilla, was born into captivity at the San Francisco Zoo. Amazingly, Koko was taught how to use sign language to communicate and throughout her life, she could make more than **1,000 SIGNS AND UNDERSTAND UP TO 2,000 SPOKEN WORDS.**

In the wild, gorillas don't have anywhere near the vocabulary Koko had. But scientists have found that the animals use their faces to talk to each other. When they want to play, a gorilla will open its mouth wide, with the lips covering its teeth. It's a dopey look, but it tells the others that they'd like to have fun.

THE SAUSALITO HUM →

In the 1980s, people living on yachts in the San Francisco Bay started to experience something weird as the sun set over their city. Each evening, as they laid their heads down to sleep, they noticed a horrible humming creeping in through the hulls of their houseboats. The sound was so loud, it actually kept people up at night.

Some thought the constant droning sound was the work of a secret military project. Others said aliens were to blame. But several decades later, the true source of the so-called Sausalito Hum was revealed to be none other than a bunch of grumpy-faced fish looking for love. TOADFISH, TO BE EXACT.

→ With a flat face like a frog, slimy skin and gnarly, whiskery-looking barbels that hang off of its lower jaw, THE TOADFISH ISN'T EXACTLY WHAT YOU'D CALL BEAUTIFUL. But what it lacks in looks, it more than makes up in loudness.

→ Toadfish are one of the many species of fish that can sing even though they live underwater. It does so by making muscles next to its bladder vibrate at speeds as fast as 300 TIMES PER SECOND. That's faster than the fastest hummingbird can beat its wings!

To us, the toadfish's song sounds a bit like a vibrating phone left on a table. But to other toadfish, each call is a complex symphony of two basic notes, which scientists call grunts and boops. **EACH FISH CAN ARRANGE ITS NOTES IN DIFFERENT COMBINATIONS** to create unique songs that attract mates and warn other toadfish to stay off its turf.

→ Scientists have also found that a toadfish will grunt loudly in the middle of its neighbors' songs, probably as an attempt to mess them up. **IN OTHER WORDS, SOME TOADFISH ARE RUDE.**

THE WORLD'S MOST IMPRESSIVE COPYCAT IS A BIRD

If you're ever walking through the forests of south Australia and you hear a car alarm, don't worry—it probably isn't a robbery. To find a mate, the male lyrebird performs an elaborate repertoire, **MIMICKING THE WHISTLES, TWEETS, AND CAWS OF OTHER BIRDS, AS WELL AS COMPLEX, NON-NATURAL NOISES, LIKE A CAR ALARM!** From buzzing chainsaws to crying babies, camera shutters, gunshots, and even ringtones, the bird seems to experiment with any sound it's heard that seems interesting. And later, a lyrebird will teach its favorite sounds to its chicks—just like a parent teaching its child a nursery rhyme!

CICADAS SING WITH THEIR GUTS

If you were to go outside and yell your head off, the sound would travel less than 700 feet. And while that's loud enough to annoy your neighbor, it's nothing compared to the cicada, whose **100-DECIBEL DRONE CAN TRAVEL MORE THAN 1 MILE.** And the little critter doesn't even have any vocal chords or lungs!

Instead, the male cicada uses the noisemaker organs on the sides of its belly known as tymbals. Each time it flexes its muscles, the series of ribs and membranes inside its tymbals click, a bit like straightening and scrunching up a bendy straw . . . hundreds of times per second!

SHAKE, RATTLE, AND ROLL →

Many of the ways animals communicate with each other are secretive or complex. Others are quick—blink and you might miss them—or completely invisible, as is the case with chemical signaling. But not the rattlesnake. When the rattlesnake has something to say, it just shakes the maraca glued to its tail, and the whole world stops to listen.

A rattlesnake's musical instrument is made up of a series of hollow segments at the end of its tail that make noise when they vibrate against each other. Many people are terrified of hearing the distinctive *SHH-SHH-SHH* of a rattlesnake's rattle while they're walking in the woods. And no wonder: There are thirty-six species of rattlesnakes native to the Americas, and while they are all slightly different, they each possess large, backward-curving fangs capable of injecting a potent cocktail of venom that can knock a human down dead.

WHEN DANGER CALLS, BEAVERS GET SLAPPY

Many things make beavers awesome—like unbreakable teeth and waterproof fur—but their tails might be the best. Large, flat and paddle-like, rough to the touch and covered in black scales, a beaver's tail is used as a rudder in the water, an extra leg on land, a fat store and a handy, built-in **TAIL-E-PHONE!**

When a beaver detects a threat, it raises its tail above the water and slaps it down hard. This *THWACK* is heard far and wide as a warning signal to other nearby beavers. And with oversize lungs that allow a beaver to remain hidden underwater for fifteen minutes . . . by the time a predator hears the *THWACK*, it's already lost its lunch.

→ But, if you think about it, we should actually be thanking the rattlesnakes. That's because rattlesnakes don't want to bite a person or another predator. Frankly, it's a waste of venom, and they'd much prefer to save that deadly potion for a mouse, squirrel, or some other tasty morsel. When a snake shakes its rattle at someone on a trail, **WHAT IT'S REALLY SAYING IS . . .**

"HEY YOU, YOU'RE SCARING ME. BUT I'M SCARY, TOO. COME ANY CLOSER, AND I'M GOING TO HAVE TO DO SOMETHING ABOUT IT."

→ How do we know this? First, because **RATTLESNAKES DON'T SHAKE THEIR TAILS AT THINGS THEY WANT TO EAT**—that would give away the surprise. And second, because if you step away from a rattlesnake, it doesn't chase after you. When it comes to people, these "nope ropes" just want to be left alone. We should probably listen to them.

THE SURPRISINGLY SNEEZY LIVES OF DEER

When most people think about deer, they picture a silent buck standing in an open field as the light fades or a doe and her fawn sipping water quietly beside a babbling brook. What most people usually don't imagine is all the **SNORTING**.

While a deer's snort-sneeze might sound silly, this loud, nasal *WHOOSH* can be pretty frightening when it catches you off guard—and might also spook a predator and cause it to run away. A snort also clears its nasal passages, allowing it to use its scent receptors to determine if the threat is worth running away from.

COCKROACHES WITH ATTITUDE

The characteristic *HISS* of the Madagascar hissing cockroach is created as it **PUSHES AIR OUT OF ITS SPIRACLES**—tiny holes found along the cockroaches body that allow air to get inside. Cockroaches need oxygen just as much as you do! And just like you, they need to breathe out after breathing in. Because the air is being forced through a tiny space—the spiracles—it creates a loud sound that the cockroach can use to scare away predators. The males also make hissing sounds as a way to attract females. To mimic this lovesong, simply try blowing hard into a drinking straw.

DO WOLVES REALLY HOWL AT THE MOON? →

The *AH-AH-AOOOOOO* of a grey wolf's howl may well be the most recognizable sound in the animal kingdom. But it's also probably the most misunderstood.

The idea that wolves howl at the moon has been bouncing around for thousands of years. But the truth is, there's no evidence that wolves vocalize at the moon or that they use Earth's big, bright satellite as anything more than a source of light on an otherwise dark night. But grey wolves do howl quite a bit, and there's a good reason for it.

→ Wolves are social animals which usually run in packs of five to twelve—but that can sometimes range upwards of thirty individuals. And in these large packs, **HOWLING IS AN IMPORTANT FORM OF COMMUNICATION.**

→ Experts believe wolves use their howls to do everything from **COORDINATING HUNTS** to **FINDING EACH OTHER IN SNOWSTORMS.** Howls can tell the rest of the entourage that there's a nice moose carcass nearby, or they can be used to warn rival packs that they're intruding on occupied territory.

→ **IT DOES SEEM TO BE TRUE THAT WOLF PACKS HOWL MORE OFTEN AT NIGHT,** which may seem eerie, but this is probably just because wolves hunt mostly at night—not because they want to haunt your dreams.

DHOLES WHISTLE WHILE THEY WORK

Some people describe the dhole (pronunciation hint: the *h* is silent) as sort of a mix between a grey fox and a red fox, but the animals are more closely related to their African counterparts than the rest of the canine family tree. With reddish fur and pointy snouts, the dhole is also known as the **WHISTLING DOG** because it communicates through dense brush by creating a series of **SHORT, SHRILL WHISTLES**. But that's not all. The animals can produce a sort of **COO-COO**, as well as an attack cry that sounds like **KAKAKAKA!** Truthfully, the dhole sounds more like a bird than any hound you've ever met.

THE WORLD'S LOUDEST LAND ANIMAL

There's a species of monkey in the rainforests of Central and South America that is so loud that everyone calls them **HOWLER MONKEYS**. The world's loudest land animal can be heard close to 3 miles away, thanks to a big, hollow, U-shaped bone in its throat—known as the hyoid—which amplifies its roar.

A howler's vocalizations advertises how **BIG AND BAD** it is to all the other males in the area. So, in other words, instead of duking it out in the treetops, which could lead to injury or even death, howlers first try to settle their wars with words. Just . . . **REALLY, REALLY LOUD WORDS!**

SAYING IT WITH A SNEEZE . . .

African wild dogs can form packs of more than twenty dogs at a time. And when one gets hungry, a hunt gets voted on . . . by sneezing, of course! The dogs start by touching each other's heads, wagging their tails, and running back and forth. Then, someone starts sneezing. **THE MORE DOGS THAT JOIN IN THE SNEEZE PARTY, THE MORE LIKELY IT IS THAT THE GROUP WILL TAKE OFF IN SEARCH OF PREY.** Interestingly, it seems as if not every sneeze counts the same; a pack leader's might just take three, while a lower-ranking member could take up to ten sneezes for everyone to join in.

SIZE, SHAPE, SPEED, COLOR: THE PRAIRIE DOG VOCABULARY

Some scientists believe that prairie dogs possess a vocabulary of **PIPS, SQUEAKS, AND CHIRPS** so advanced that they can actually describe the physical appearance of a threat, **BARKING IN A CODE**. When scientists walked through a prairie dog colony wearing white lab coats, the animals made mostly the same alarm call. But when those same scientists put on blue, grey, orange, and green T-shirts, the talkative rodents made different squeaks altogether. Which might make you want to dress up a little bit the next time you go for a hike on the prairie . . . Who knows what those little rodents will say behind your back!

OUR CLOSEST COUSINS ARE CHATTERBOXES ↓

In the forests of West Africa, there are these trees . . . weird trees—hollow trunks, with their bark scratched off and piles of stones found at their base. Trees, of course, do not collect rocks. And neither do birds or elephants or even the local people who live there. So, how did the stones get inside the tree hollows? Chimpanzees.

Using camera traps, scientists have seen four different populations of chimps go up to these trees and **FLING ROCKS** the size of their own heads at them. Again and again, the chimps stop by, throw a rock, yell out a little pant-hoot sound, and then they sit, and they wait.

According to the cameras, the chimps receive nothing from the behavior. That is, it's not as if the act of chucking rocks at a tree knocks down some juicy fruit or opens up a honeybee hive. Nor does the activity, which scientists call accumulative stone throwing, appear to be some fun game that chimps do together.

The scientists' best guess is that this thunky echo represents some sort of chimpanzee **LONG-DISTANCE COMMUNICATION**. What the chimps are saying remains anyone's guess.

→ There's more and more reason to believe our closest cousins in the animal kingdom are **CAPABLE OF COMMUNICATING COMPLEX THOUGHTS AND IDEAS WITH EACH OTHER IN A WAY THAT OTHER ANIMALS CANNOT.** Scientists know, for instance, that chimpanzees will call each other over when food is found, using a series of pant-hoots, grunts, and barks. Likewise, a loud **WRAAAA** call is a heads-up to the rest of the troop that something different, interesting or dangerous is nearby. And each individual chimpanzee can be seen performing his or her own unique pant-hoot sound that sets the individual apart from the rest of the group. It's not quite a name, but it's also not far off.

→ MALES CAN BE ESPECIALLY EXPRESSIVE, making loud noises and aggressive displays to show all the other guys nearby who's boss. Typical moves include slapping the ground or trees with their hands, stomping their feet, running around and dragging big branches, and even throwing rocks.

→ GESTURES ARE ALSO INCREDIBLY IMPORTANT FOR THE PRIMATES. When a mother chimp raises her hind foot, it seems to tell her baby that it's fine to hop on for a piggyback ride. And when another chimp is getting too close, a little push with the back of the hand signals that he or she wants some space. Chimps can also be seen repeatedly tearing leaves into strips with their teeth, almost like a person nervously chewing on a pencil, and this is thought to be an invitation to flirt.

→ Maybe even more interestingly, another study—there are a lot of people studying chimpanzees!—found that human toddlers make fifty-two different gestures to communicate, and forty-six of them have also been seen being used by chimpanzees. **PERHAPS WE'RE EVEN MORE SIMILAR THAN MOST OF US REALIZE!**

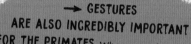

ELEPHANTS HAVE EARTHSHAKING CONVERSATIONS →

Elephants communicate with infrasounds—waves that are so far down on the frequency scale that they are also outside a human's range of hearing. These sounds are made by passing air across the animal's vocal cords, the same way that humans sing. The only difference is that the elephant's vocal cords are eight times larger than ours, so the sound that comes out is lower in frequency.

→ Now, here's the really interesting part. BECAUSE ELEPHANT SOUND WAVES ARE SO LOW, AND SO LOUD, THEY CAN ACTUALLY TRAVEL THROUGH THE GROUND for up to 6 miles, kind of like a mini-version of how an earthquake sends shock waves through the Earth. In fact, scientists are able to measure elephant infrasound using a device known as a seismometer, which is the same thing they use to measure earthquakes!

THE TARSIER'S SILENT SCREAM

One day, a team of researchers was watching some Philippine tarsiers in the lab, when they noticed the animals opening their mouths—but no sound came out, almost as if they were yawning. Curious, they used a special sound recorder and discovered the critters weren't yawning at all. They were **SCREAMING**.

Tarsiers, it seems, are the world's only primates to screech in ultrasound, or pitches so high the human ear can't even register them as noise. Moths and katydids—some of the tarsier's favorite foods—also make sounds in the ultrasonic range. That means tarsiers may well be using **ULTRASOUND TO SEND SECRET MESSAGES**—undetectable by their predators—but also as a shortcut for finding dinner.

SLAPPING NOSTRILS: A DOLPHIN TALE

The dolphin is famous for its ability to echolocate, or "see" objects by producing clicks and then listening to the echoes that bounce back. It produces these clicks by slapping its nostrils—which are way up inside their head—against other fatty parts of its nasal cavity. But did you know it can communicate using those same parts, only sped up really, really quickly?

When a dolphin wants to use echolocation, it produces sounds at around 20 clicks per second. But when a dolphin wants to talk, it makes sounds at around 2,000 clicks per second. Scientists call the first kind of sound **ECHOLOCATION CLICKS**, while the second kind are known as **BURST PULSES**.

Dolphins use burst pulses for all kinds of things. Want to play? Send out a burst pulse. Feeling anxious? Burst pulse. Want to annoy or even intimidate another dolphin? A burst pulse might even be able to be used as a weapon, just like a really loud scream right into the eardrum. Scientists have even seen mother dolphins directing burst pulses at their babies, or calves, when they are misbehaving!

→ But, you may be wondering, how does an elephant hear a message that's traveling through the ground? Well, with its feet, of course! Elephants have enormous feet. Everyone knows that. But what most people don't realize is THESE PILLAR-LIKE FEET ARE PACKED WITH DOZENS OF SENSORY RECEPTORS THAT ARE SENSITIVE TO VIBRATIONS.

→ Elephants even have the ability to flatten and squish those huge, fatty feet down into the soil, allowing them to pick up seismic vibrations, similar to the way you might cup a hand to your ear to hear better—YOU'RE TAKING A BODY PART BUILT FOR CATCHING SOUND WAVES AND MAKING IT BIGGER, if only temporarily.

→ Amazingly, some scientists believe we can help protect elephants from poachers by developing a network of devices that could eavesdrop or listen in on their infrasound. When ALARM CALLS OR STAMPEDE SOUNDS are recorded at an odd hour of the night, rangers could then be dispatched to the location to make sure the elephants aren't in danger.

FARTING FISH: YES, SERIOUSLY

When a herring wants to talk to another herring, it BLOWS BUBBLES OUT OF ITS BACKSIDE that make a series of loud pops. Scientists call these interesting sounds Fast, Repetitive Ticks, or FRTs. Farts. Herring talk to each other using farts.

You see, water is a good conductor of sound, which means that sound waves can travel five times faster than through the air, and herring appear to use it to send WARNINGS AND OTHER MESSAGES. So, what sounds like a bunch of teenagers making noises with their hands under their armpits may actually be a serious signal that helps herring stay alive.

SQUEAKS AND SQUAWKS
ARE HOW THE BATS SEE AND TALK ↓

Do you remember how tarsiers make calls in ultrasound—sounds that are so high in frequency people can't hear them? Well, bats do the same thing. Only better.

That's because not only can bats produce CHIRPS AND SQUEAKS of incredibly high frequencies, but they can actually hear when those sound waves bump off something out in the night and then bounce back. And they can use those sounds to navigate in tight spaces, such as caves, or to pick off insects in midair, like a fighter jet.

Scientists have only recently discovered that while echolocation squeaks are important for hunting, they are also used to communicate. Mexican free-tailed bats and greater horseshoe bats have been found to emit identification calls, for example. And this makes sense, because some bat species are known to roost in colonies of millions of other bats. The identification calls are how the bats yell out to the rest of the colony, "HEY! IT'S ME!"

Greater sac-winged bats can also determine the sex of another bat based solely on its squeaks, and they respond differently based on that information. When a male heard another male echolocating, it would send out aggressive calls. But if the same bat heard a female echolocating, it would start making more social sounds.

With the amount that has been discovered only recently, there's clearly a lot we still don't know about how bat echolocation works. But it's already squarely in the realm of a superpower.

→ Bats can do some amazing things with their echoey clicks. For instance, they can determine HOW BIG AN INSECT IS based on how strong the rebounding waves are, whether it's above or below them, to the right or the left, and even whether it's flying toward or away from them.

→ Some bats make these high-pitched sounds with their mouths, while others make it inside their noses. **SOME FRUIT BATS HAVE EVEN BEEN ABLE TO USE THE SOUNDS MADE BY THEIR WINGS** to perform a much simpler form of echolocation. (Though most fruit bats are still thought not to echolocate much at all. Which makes sense, if you think about it. Their prey—fruit—doesn't move around all that much!)

→ Leaf-nosed bats can use echolocation to spot dragonflies resting on a leaf in the middle of the rainforest, which means a target doesn't even have to be moving for a bat to zero in on it. (Scientists say the leaf acts like a mirror, reflecting the bat's calls back to them.) **SOME BATS CAN EVEN "SEE" TEXTURES USING ONLY SOUND!**

→ All of this is accomplished with highly specialized ears that can pick up the slightest of echoes. And you can get a taste of how it works by closing your eyes, clapping and slowly walking around your house—though please avoid any stairs! Hallways with an open doorway are best. Can you hear how the claps sound louder and faster when you're standing near a wall? Or how the claps sound farther away when you step in front of the opening doorway? **THAT'S ECHOLOCATION! YOU'RE ECHOLOCATING!**

→ With echolocation, bulldog bats can spot the ripples made by minnows on the surface of the water and actually snatch the baby fish up using their feet, just like a bald eagle. **(THAT'S RIGHT, BATS GO FISHING!)**

SHAKE YOUR TAIL FEATHER ↓

Everybody knows that birds can produce a variety of noises. Songbirds sing, turkeys gobble, penguins trill, ducks quack, and owls hoot. But did you know some birds can make sounds using only their feathers? To put it in human terms, that would be like using your hair to sing.

→ Common nighthawks perform a display in which they look and sound like a **TINY FIGHTER JET SWOOPING PAST.**

→ Hummingbirds are especially good feather-singers. When a male wants to impress a female, he will fly high into the forest canopy, then he'll turn and dive quickly in her direction. Like a bullet, the bird falls out of the sky, gaining more and more speed until, **AT THE VERY LAST SECOND, HE FANS OUT HIS TAIL FEATHERS.** This creates friction with the air and causes the edges of the hummingbird's feathers to vibrate and make noise, kind of like when you blow on a blade of grass held between your fingers.

WHAT HAPPENS WHEN YOU GIVE AN ALLIGATOR HELIUM?

Lots of children want to be astronauts when they grow up because it could mean a trip to space. But, if that doesn't work out, you might want to consider becoming a biologist. Because they sometimes give helium to alligators!

Researchers placed a talkative captive Chinese alligator in a sound chamber to record her normal calls—loud, low rumbles. Then they pumped her enclosure full of heliox (oxygen mixed with helium) and again recorded the calls. The researcher's computer deduced that these calls had come from a smaller alligator. The scientists think this means that **GATORS CAN USE THESE SOUNDS TO SIZE EACH OTHER UP,** either for evaluating a rival in mating season, or perhaps for avoiding costly fights altogether.

THE CALL OF THE DRUMMER

Each spring, the woodpecker's delightful **RAT-A-TAT-TAT** echoes through the forest. But wait. **RAT-A-TAT-TAT.** Is the sound getting closer? Just going to look out the window and see if—yes, that woodpecker isn't drilling into a tree anymore. It's on the side of the house, banging its bill against the gutters. Now it's on a telephone pole . . . now the chimney . . . all places with no juicy insects, but that offer the woodpecker something else—**A MICROPHONE.** You see, many woodpecker species also use drumming as a way to attract mates or claim territory. And louder, longer drums signal to all the other woodpeckers around that this drummer means business.

→ When a predator gets too close to a crested pigeon, the bird's wings produce an **ALARM CALL** as it flies away that warns all the other pigeons that there is danger lurking nearby.

→ The ruffed grouse may be the most interesting wing-singer of all. During mating season, the male hops up on a log in the middle of the woods and starts to flap its wings in a way that kind of looks like a gorilla beating its chest. The first few strokes are slow, but within a few seconds, the bird is flapping so fast, it produces a loud drumming that can be heard far and wide. In fact, **HIKERS OFTEN MISTAKE THE RUFFED GROUSE'S MATING CALL FOR THE SOUND A CHAIN SAW OR LAWN MOWER MAKES!**

THE MOST METAL MOLE RATS ON EARTH

Straight up antisocial, all the northeast African mole rat really wants is for everyone to just get out of its face. Now, you might think this misanthropic miner wouldn't care much for communication. But, when this mole rat hears another tunneling too close to its own burrow, it will start **KNOCKING ITS NOGGIN** against the roof of its home, much like an old man banging his ceiling with a broom. Scientists call this seismic communication, since it creates vibrations that travel through the soil. But you can call it **HEADBANGING**.

FROM SINGING KATYDIDS TO HISSING TARANTULAS ↓

The Goliath birdeater is a tarantula that hails from South America. These suckers weigh more than a McDonald's Quarter Pounder and have fangs that can be more than 1 inch long, which makes them the heaviest and gnarliest spider on Earth. Oh, and as their name suggests, they sometimes snatch and devour birds.

Yes, you read that right—THERE ARE SPIDERS THAT EAT BIRDS.

Of course, even though the Goliath birdeater is massive for an arachnid, the animals are still much smaller than many other hungry mouths in the rainforest. Which is why these spiders have a trick to scare predators away before they get into a fight and wind up losing a few legs, or worse.

When a Goliath birdeater is backed into a corner, it QUICKLY RUBS THE HAIRS ON ITS FRONT LEGS TOGETHER TO CREATE A LOUD, SPOOKY HISS. Unlike a cat's HISS or a dog's SNARL, this sound has nothing to do with the movement of air. Instead, what a predator hears is friction.

This is what scientists call stridulation, and it's the preferred noisemaking trick among all kinds of creepy-crawlies. Crickets, katydids, and grasshoppers are among the most famous stridulators, but others include longhorn beetles, velvet ants, water boatmen, and even some millipedes and crustaceans, like the rock lobster.

Stridulation is a little bit different in each animal, but it usually follows the same premise. One piece of the body is rubbed against another in a way that it sticks and slips in rapid succession. THIS CREATES VIBRATION, AND VIBRATION CREATES SOUND.

→ By the way, invertebrates (creatures without a spine) don't get to have all the stridulating fun. **TENRECS**—which are creatures native to Madagascar and similar to hedgehogs—can actually create **ULTRASOUND** by rubbing their spines together, and scientists believe these sounds are used to communicate with each other while foraging.

→ The **CLUB-WINGED MANAKIN**, a bird species that lives in Andean cloud forests, can vibrate its feathers so fast, it creates a stridulation sound that can be mistaken for **SINGING**.

→ And then there's the **SAW-SCALED VIPER**, a venomous snake found across Asia and Africa. When this serpent gets riled up, it slithers against itself in the shape of a flowing S. As the snake scratches its scales up against each other, they produce an **AUDIBLE WARNING HISS**, not unlike the Goliath birdeater on the other side of the Atlantic Ocean.

SMELL AND TASTE

DON'T EAT THE YELLOW SNOW ↓

Anyone who has ever walked a dog knows a little bit about how animals communicate using chemicals. Of course, to us, it can just look like a lot of peeing.

You see, every time a dog lifts its leg on a tree trunk or patch of begonias, it's adding a signature to canine social media. This is because URINE CONTAINS CHEMICALS KNOWN AS PHEROMONES that communicate all kinds of interesting information. By sniffing these scent markings, a dog can learn whether the animal that left the splatter was male or female, and whether they are available to mate. The age of the scent marking may also reveal how long it's been since another dog came through the area, and the height at which the marking is made gives a hint about the size of the dog that left it.

So, the next time you take your dog for a walk, try not to get annoyed if it seems to want to sniff every single blade of grass along the way. YOUR DOG IS JUST SCROLLING THROUGH CANINE SOCIAL MEDIA!

→ In South America, a distant relative of the modern dog takes this one step further. Known as the BUSH DOG, this clever, little jungle dweller PERFORMS A SORT OF HANDSTAND when marking its territory. It stands on its front paws while spraying urine all over the thing it wants to mark. It's not completely clear why bush dogs perform a handstand, but we do know that the animals are incredibly secretive.

FISH CAN'T TALK, SO THEY PEE INSTEAD

When a **CICHLID** gets into disputes with its rivals, the little terrors swim right up to their enemies in an aggressive manner, with fins raised, and let loose a **CLOUD OF CHEMICAL-LADEN URINE.**

→ It's likely that scent markings play a large role in bush dog communication, and doing a handstand might give the bush dogs a **LEG UP**, so to speak, because higher scent markings would have a better chance of catching the wind. In turn, this would make it easier for bush dogs to smell the pheromone-laced urine from farther away.

→ Smaller dogs tend to lift their legs higher than bigger dogs, perhaps because this angles their urine stream up into the air. And while scientists aren't completely sure why this is the case, one theory has it that the small dogs are telling a bit of a fib with their scent markings. By spraying its urine high up on tree trunk, **A SMALL DOG MIGHT BE ABLE TO TRICK OTHER DOGS** into thinking its markings came from a big dog.

PORCUPINE COURTSHIP: A SMELLY AFFAIR

Urine plays an important role in the lives of porcupines in North America, but not in battles. In an attempt to mate with a female, a male porcupine will rear up on his hind legs and **SPRAY URINE AT THE FEMALE.**

Scientists have found that for some animals, pheromones present in urine can kick-start the female's reproductive system.

SAY IT, DON'T SPRAY IT

Leopards use their urine to send a message to others in the savannah: **THIS IS MY TURF.** They sniff at the air, flick their tail out of the way, clench their backside and shoot a stream of urine onto the trunk of the nearest acacia tree. And did you know that their urine smells a bit like buttered popcorn?

GIRAFFE COURTSHIP: A TASTY AFFAIR

If a giraffe wants to get a sense of whether a female is ready to mate, a male giraffe will actually **TASTE** the female's urine. Apparently, chemical receptors in the giraffe's mouth can pick up on pheromones that signal reproductive availability. This is pretty cool from a scientific perspective, but makes you glad you're not a giraffe.

THE SPLASH ZONE →

If you ever go to the zoo, be careful not to stand too close to a hippopotamus. Not because they can grow to weigh as much as 4 tons or move at speeds approaching 19 miles per hour, though both statistics are impressive. No, you'll want to be careful because these semiaquatic herbivores can fling their feces (poo) up to 6.5 feet through the air. Get too close and you'll be smack dab in the middle of the SPLASH ZONE!

FOR SOME ANIMALS, NUMBER 2 IS THE NUMBER 1

White rhinos put all their poo in the same place, called a dung midden. At more than 65 feet in length, these piles of poo can stretch the **LENGTH OF 1.5 SCHOOL BUSES** parked end to end. When scientists analyzed the chemicals found in rhinoceros middens, they learned that adult male rhinos spend time sniffing the piles left behind by females who were ready to mate. A midden sniff is actually more like a message board for rhinos to keep with one another's news.

ODD SHAPES

Wombats, a type of buck-toothed marsupial, use middens to mark the edges of their territories. Wombat poo piles are extra special, because these curious critters are the only known animals on Earth that **POOS OUT CUBES**.

→ Hippos accomplish this yucky feat by **USING THEIR TAILS LIKE A PROPELLER**. As the poo exits the animals' backside, it hits the tail and launches into the air in all directions.

→ Why do hippos do this, when other herbivores like cows and deer just let their scat go splat? Well, just like some animals use urine as a calling card, other animals choose to use poo. And if you're going to use poo to send messages, then it makes sense for you to be able to **BLAST THOSE MESSAGES FAR AND WIDE.**

ARASITE ARANOIA

e dik-dik, an frican antelope, ay use middens as a ay to avoid intestinal arasites. Studies have own that the animal careful not to nibble ants near its middens, erhaps because ose areas have more **ARASITES LURKING THE GRASS.**

TASTY DUNG HEAPS

The toilet areas used by tapirs, which eat fruit and seeds, make for critical rainforest regeneration sites, since some plant seeds can survive the animal's digestive tract and take root in the nutrient-rich dung heap.

INGRAM'S SQUIRRELS

have been found to search for tapir droppings because they know there's food to be found there.

WHAT'S BLACK AND WHITE AND STINKY ALL OVER? →

Quick, name a smelly animal.

Did you pick the skunk? You did, didn't you? And for good reason! Skunks have a reputation for squirting a liquid out of their backsides that stinks. The **NOXIOUS SMELL** present in skunk spray is made up of seven parts, three of which are thiols, three are thioacetates, and the final part is an alkaloid. But you don't have to know their names to know what they create. In no uncertain terms, skunk spray is a pungent and nauseating odor.

→ Skunks are neither large nor particularly dangerous. Their teeth and claws are tiny. And yet, they have found a way to send predators packing simply by stacking a few hydrogen and sulfur atoms together and then **SPEWING THEM OUT OF THEIR BUTTS** at distances of up to 10 feet.

→ A skunk has limited ammo, which means it can't just start shooting anytime an animal looks at them funny. In fact, **A SKUNK WILL USUALLY TRY TO AVOID SPRAYING AT ALL** by first going through a series of less costly warnings. These include arching the back and sticking its hair up on its end. A threatened skunk may stomp on the ground with its feet and even point its butt at an attacker. Upon seeing all of these warning signs, most animals decide to look for something else to eat.

The chemicals in a skunk's spray make your **EYES WATER** and can affect your vision. They can also cause chemical burns on an animal's skin and, if inhaled, can make you cough or gag.

SCENT TRAILS

If you've ever stopped to watch a line of **ANTS**, then you've probably wondered **HOW SO MANY KNOW WHERE TO GO** without ever uttering a peep. You see, every time a foraging ant finds something tasty to bring back to the nest, it leaves a trail of pheromones on the ground behind it as it returns. This encourages more ants to go to that food source and bring back resources. These workers will also emit alarm pheromones when the nest is under attack. With the same effect as ringing a bell, it tells the whole colony to prepare to defend itself. This is an effective strategy for social insects, who can create effective defenses against large animals like raccoons, or even bears, when they all work together.

CHEMICAL WEAPONS

Many farmers defend their fields and orchards from crop-eating **MOTHS** by catching them with sticky traps baited with female pheromones. They set up several female pheromone dispensers all over the grounds that keep the male moths busy flying back and forth. In other words, if it smells like females everywhere, then the **MALES HAVE NO WAY TO NAVIGATE** to the real potential mates. Pest control methods that use pheromones mean farmers have to spray less pesticides, which is not only better for the people eating those crops, but also the animals that live near the farms, fields, and orchards that produce them. It's a win-win. Except for all those lonely bugs, of course.

THE CRAZY, LIFE-OR-DEATH WORLD OF CATERPILLAR CHEMICALS

PARASITIC WASPS are highly sensitive to chemical cues, which allow them to sniff out tiny caterpillars hiding in the rainforest and plan an attack. But lucky for caterpillars, they have a defense plan. A caterpillar can vomit all over its attacker, covering the wasp in liquified plant matter. The vomit is full of plant toxins that cause the wasp's sensory arrays to go haywire. And the caterpillar makes a swift getaway . . .

SNAKE TONGUESSS ↓

For people with ophidiophobia, or a phobia of snakes, there's nothing creepier than the way a serpent flicks its forked tongue. In fact, some people think that when a snake sticks its tongue out, it's a warning that it will soon strike.

But what it's really doing is LICKING THE AIR.

Just like the mammals that perform the flehmen response (see right), snakes have two holes in the roof of their mouths. And when a snake reels its long tongue back inside, it actually pokes those two prongs into these holes, like a plug going into a socket. This transfers molecules it collects from the air directly to the vomeronasal organ, or Jacobson's organ, in its head so that it can better perceive the world outside.

Even cooler, the forked tongue plays a role here—depending on which prong collects the molecules, the snake can get a sense of which direction they are smelling.

Snakes rely on their olfactory sense, or sense of smell. Scents allow the reptiles to tell the difference between SOMETHING THEY CAN EAT AND SOMETHING THEY NEED TO PROTECT THEMSELVES AGAINST.

Most snake pheromones that scientists have found seem to be made out of lipids, or fats, which make the scents too heavy to travel easily through the air. Instead, snakes must actually touch their tongue to the skin of another snake to detect its pheromones, which could convey whether that particular animal is a male or female and if it's ready to mate.

→ One curious exemption to the rule that snakes must actually touch their tongues to the skin of another snake to detect its pheromones seems to be RED-SIDED GARTER SNAKES. These snakes form GIGANTIC MATING BALLS of tens of thousands of individual snakes all looking to breed.

→ One cave in Canada is thought to contain UPWARD OF 70,000 OF THESE SERPENTS each winter, for instance. And with that much competition for mates, it seems the snakes have evolved the ability to smell through the air when nearby snakes have already partnered up. This helps the snakes avoid wasting time and energy on a partner not likely to be interested in going on a snake date.

BRAIN

TONGUE NERVE

JACOBSON'S ORGAN

WHAT'S THE DEAL WITH "FUNNY CAT FACE"?

Have you ever seen your **CAT** scrunch up its nose, bare its teeth, and start to pant? While this behavior may look like kitty wants to pick a fight, it's actually a special kind of sniffing called the flehmen response. Sometimes called the lip-curl, the gape response, or even funny cat face, many mammals are known to perform this behavior. Rhinos and rams do the flehmen, as do llamas, tapirs, elk, and giraffes.

So, what's really going on here? According to scientists, the flehmen response is used by animals when they want to get a better sense of what's in the air. Two tiny pits on the roof of the mouth are linked to tubes called the nasopalatine canals, which in turn connect to a special glob of neurons called the Jacobson's organ. Weirdly, these neurons are completely different from the ones that are associated with the sense of smell. This means that when an animal is flehmening, **IT'S NOT ACTUALLY SMELLING OR TASTING, BUT DOING SOMETHING IN BETWEEN.**

Even more interesting, the flehmen response is what's known as a voluntary action. In other words, while we can't help but smell the cake sitting on the windowsill, a mouse must choose to turn on its super sniffer—sort of like a superhero's superpower.

Most animals seem to use their flehmen responses as a way to sample chemicals given off by other members of the same species, which means it's primarily a tool used for mating, marking territory, and other forms of communication. However, there's no telling how much those super schnozzes may be picking up when the flehmen is engaged.

ELECTROSENSORY AND TOUCH

A WHIP SCORPION'S TENDER CARESS ↓

Have you ever heard the expression, "if looks could kill"? That was most likely written about whip scorpions.

Whip scorpions aren't actually scorpions, they are arachnids that rank up there on the list of creepy-crawlies. They have shiny, black exoskeletons and faces that look like a Swiss Army knife of horrific appendages built for shredding insects and other tiny creatures. More technically known as amblypygids, these critters also have eight legs that are so long and spindly in some species that their "wingspans" can stretch out more than 2 feet in length. Oh, and some varieties can also spew a spicy, vinegar-like acid from their backsides earning the creatures yet another name—vinegaroons.

The thing about whip scorpions is that while they look like nightmare monsters, these arachnids are actually almost completely harmless to humans.

→ What's more, females can be very motherly with their brood. Before their little minions grow up and become adults, the mother whip scorpion and her young will move around in a pack, with the mother caressing her brood with her long, whiplike feelers. Scientists think that the whip scorpion's whips play a role in communicating with the babies, keeping them nearby, and maybe even CALMING THEM LIKE A MOTHER COOING TO HER BABY.

HOLD ME BY THE ANTENNAE

When an **ANT** wants to show another ant something interesting, like a juicy apple core, it will **TAP THE OTHER ANT** a few times with the antennae sprouting out of its head. Once it is sure it has the attention it wants, it will turn around and start walking toward the point of interest. The second ant then follows, tapping at the leader's rump with its own antennae. Indeed, if the first ant goes too fast and loses the follower, it'll realize because the second ant's tappity-taps stop. This is the ant's equivalent of leading someone by the hand.

THE ELEPHANT'S SUPER SENSOR SCHNOZ

Everybody knows the elephant's trunk. But did you know these long, flexible noses contain more than **40,000 MUSCLES**, compared to the 650 or so contained in the entire human body? Elephants are constantly using their trunks to touch, caress, and stroke other members of their groups. They will also stop to exchange touches when coming across another group of elephants, almost as if they were shaking hands. Because an elephant's trunk also contains powerful scent-processing power, it's likely that all of these touchy-feely behaviors serve a dual purpose of smelling. Imagine if you had a nose on the end of your hand!

ALLIGATOR DUNKING CONTEST

These gigantic reptiles spend their time **TESTING ONE ANOTHER'S STRENGTH** by trying to see who can dunk whom. To do so, an alligator will swim up beside a potential mate and lay its head on top of the other alligator's shoulders and head. Then, as part of its mating ritual, it presses down and tries to push its potential soulmate under the water's surface, sometimes holding the other gator underwater for up to five minutes. Scientists call this seemingly silly behavior **PRESSING**. And don't worry, an alligator can hold its breath for more than an hour, which means no one's ever in danger of running out of air!

I WANNA HOLD YOUR HAND

Sea otters are cuddly-looking, floating fur sausages native to the North Pacific Ocean. If you watch sea otters for long enough, you're likely to see them boop snoots. Touching noses is a way for the animals to maintain social relationships and it's one way touching plays a role in otter communication. Sea otters can and do fall asleep while floating on their backs, which presents a very real danger of getting caught up in the current. To combat this, otters will **HOLD HANDS** with each other to create a sort of **FUZZY RAFT**, and then take turns napping while the others **MAKE SURE THE WHOLE CREW DOESN'T GET WASHED OUT TO SEA.**

I'LL SCRATCH YOUR BACK IF YOU SCRATCH MINE ↓

Bright colors and bioluminescence can be seen from long distances. Loud noises send messages farther still. And chemical signals let animals communicate over vast distances and over longer periods of time. Of course, tactile communication—or touching—has none of those advantages. But for the animals that practice it, the rewards can be impressive.

Chimpanzees spend a lot of their day picking dirt, plant material, dead skin, and even ticks and other parasites off of the coats of their friends. And while doing so has obvious advantages for the animal that is being groomed—everyone likes to feel fresh and clean—the act of grooming can also provide benefits for the one doing the picking. This is because chimps are much more likely to share food with members of the group who have recently groomed them. It's as if grooming is looked at as a **FAVOR**, and one that can be **REDEEMED FOR YUMMY TREATS LATER.**

→ Interestingly, a chimpanzee doesn't just have to hope one of its friends will stop by and start combing through its fur. When one of the animals is really itchy, it might sidle up to another member of the troop and offer its arm as if to say, **"I WOULDN'T MIND IF SOMEONE WANTED TO START GROOMING ME."** Similarly, chimps have been seen making long, loud, exaggerated scratches on themselves, almost like an actor in a game of charades. And these pantomimes seem to tell nearby chimps that they would like some grooming time.

→ This is known as **REFERENTIAL GESTURING**, and it's a pretty rare thing to see among non-human animals. Think of it like this: When someone hugs themselves and says, "Brr," you know that the person is cold, even though they haven't actually said, "I'm cold."

IT'S ELECTRIC! ↓

Imagine being able to talk to a friend in the next room by shooting electricity from your fingertips.

Technically, that's what you do every time you use a smart phone . . . But did you know a whole bunch of fish can perform the same magic trick using nothing but their guts?

Everybody's heard of the electric eel—which, by the way, is not really an eel, but a species of knifefish, which are closely related to catfish. ("Electric catfish" just doesn't have the same ring to it though, does it?) Electric eels are what's known as strongly electric fish. These fish are capable of generating enough volts to ZAP anything around them. Whether it's a crocodile trying to eat the electric fish for dinner or another fish that the eel wants to eat, the effect of all that underwater voltage is that the target animal's muscles seize up, PARALYZING IT, which gives the shocker a few moments to either make an escape or slurp up an easy meal.

Electric eels are just one of the species of fish capable of producing charges with specially evolved electric organs. There are also what's known as weakly electric fish, like the **BROWN GHOST KNIFEFISH**, which don't pack the power of a Taser, but instead use soft pulses of electricity to explore the underwater world around them.

Both strongly and weakly electric fish can use their electrical fields like a kind of **SONAR**, mapping what's nearby. But they can also identify other animals around them, even when they're buried in the mud or sand, by zeroing in on the electric signatures these animals create.

All of these fish are able to use those same **ZIPS** and **ZAPS** to sense and communicate with other members of their own species, especially when it comes to reproduction. Electrical communication becomes especially important in places where visibility is low or nonexistent, like the turbid, murky waters found in the electric eel's home turf of the Amazon River in South America.

INDEX

The illustrations were created digitally
Set in Itim, Bocadillo and Magical Brush

Library of Congress Control Number 2020943686
ISBN 978-1-4197-5211-7

How To Talk To A Tiger . . . And Other Animals © 2021 Magic Cat Publishing Ltd
Written by Jason Bittel
Illustrations copyright © 2021 Kelsey Buzzell
Book design by Nicola Price
Edited by Jenny Broom
Cover © 2021 Magic Cat

Printed and bound in China
10 9 8 7 6 5 4 3 2 1

Abrams Books are available at special discounts when purchased in quantity for premiums and promotions
as well as fundraising or educational use. Special editions can also be created to specification. For details, contact
specialsales@abramsbooks.com or the address below.

ABRAMS The Art of Books
195 Broadway, New York, NY 10007
abramsbooks.com